LINDSEY VONN

BY RYAN NAGELHOUT

Gareth Stevens
PUBLISHING

Please visit our website, www.garethstevens.com. For a free color catalog of all our high-quality books, call toll free 1-800-542-2595 or fax 1-877-542-2596.

Library of Congress Cataloging-in-Publication Data

Names: Nagelhout, Ryan.
Title: Lindsey Vonn / Ryan Nagelhout.
Description: New York : Gareth Stevens Publishing, [2016] | Series: Sports MVPs | Includes index.
Identifiers: LCCN 2016009789 | ISBN 9781482446456 (paperback) | ISBN 9781482446418 (library bound) | ISBN 9781482449655 (6 pack)
Subjects: LCSH: Vonn, Lindsey–Juvenile literature. | Skiers–United States–Biography–Juvenile literature.
Classification: LCC GV854.2.V66 N34 2016 | DDC 796.93092–dc23
LC record available at http://lccn.loc.gov/2016009789

Published in 2017 by
Gareth Stevens Publishing
111 East 14th Street, Suite 349
New York, NY 10003

Copyright © 2017 Gareth Stevens Publishing

Designer: Samantha DeMartin
Editor: Ryan Nagelhout

Photo credits: Cover, p. 1 Mitch Gunn/Shutterstock.com; p. 5 B. Stefanov/Shutterstock.com; p. 7 Agence Zoom/3rd Party-Agents/Getty Images; p. 9 PAOLO COCCO/AFP/Getty Images; p. 11 (inset) Brian Bahr/Getty Images Sport/Getty Images; pp. 11 (main), 13 Agence Zoom/Getty Images Sport/Getty Images; pp. 15, 21 (World Cup) Alain Grosclaude/Agence Zoom/Getty Images Sport/Getty Images; p. 17 (left) Clive Rose/Getty Images Sport/Getty Images; p. 17 (right) Clive Mason/Getty Images Sport/Getty Images; p. 19 Mitchell Gunn/Getty Images Sport/Getty Images; p. 21 (ESPY) Kevin Mazur/WireImage/Getty Images; p. 21 (trophies) Incomible/Shutterstock.com.

Printed in the United States of America

CPSIA compliance information: Batch #CS16GS: For further information contact Gareth Stevens, New York, New York at 1-800-542-2595.

CONTENTS

Boldface words appear in the glossary.

Ski Superstar

Lindsey Vonn is the most successful female race skier of all time. She's also an American Olympic hero! Vonn has trained hard and won lots of **trophies** over the years. Let's learn more about this skiing superstar.

Minnesota Born

Vonn was born Lindsey Kildow on October 18, 1984, in St. Paul, Minnesota. She first started skiing when she was 2. Her father, Alan, and grandfather were both **competitive** skiers. Her dad even worked as her coach. She traveled to Vail, Colorado, to train.

In the Race

In the late 1990s, her parents moved Vonn, her brothers, and sister to Vail full time. She was able to train a lot harder there. Vonn started racing other skiers when she was 7. By 9, she was competing in **international** events.

9

Wins and World Cups

At 14, Vonn became the first American woman to win Italy's Trofeo Topolino event. In 2000, Vonn raced in her first World Cup. She was only 16! Her first International Ski Federation win came in 2001.

Big Firsts

Vonn competed for Team USA in the 2002 Olympics. In 2004, Vonn won her first World Cup event. She trained very hard, even learning to speak German. This made travel in other countries easier. Her career started to take off!

The Five Events

Vonn is very good at skiing different kinds of events. In 2012, she became one of six women to win World Cup events in all five kinds of alpine skiing: downhill, super G, slalom, giant slalom, and super combined.

Olympic Gold

Vonn crashed out of her second Olympics in 2006. In the 2010 Olympics, she competed in all five skiing events. Vonn won gold in the downhill and bronze in the super G. She also broke a finger in a crash!

World Champion

Vonn has won skiing's overall World Cup **championship** four times. She won 3 years in a row from 2008 to 2010 and again in 2012. In 2013, she hurt her knee and missed the 2014 Olympics. But Vonn worked hard to get back on the slopes in 2015.

Still Setting Records

In 2016, Vonn set a record with her 37th World Cup downhill win. "It's pretty awesome," Vonn said. "The more people talk about records, the harder it is to break them." Vonn plans to ski in the next Olympics, too. What records will she break next?

TROPHY CASE

**Super G
Bronze Medal**

2010 Olympics

**USOC
sportswoman
of the year**

2010

ESPY for Best Female Athlete

2010 2011

**Overall World
Cup Champion**

2008 2009
2010 2012

**Downhill
Gold Medal**

2010 Olympics

GLOSSARY

championship: the contest to decide the overall winner

competitive: having to do with working against others for the same prize

international: involving two or more countries

trophy: a prize given for winning

FOR MORE INFORMATION

BOOKS

Allen, Kathy. *Girls Race! Amazing Tales of Women in Sports.* Mankato, MN: Capstone Press, 2014.

Dann, Sarah. *Lindsey Vonn.* New York, NY: Crabtree Publishing Company, 2014.

Gitlin, Marty. *Lindsey Vonn.* Detroit, MI: Lucent Books, 2012.

WEBSITES

Alpine Athletes: Lindsey Vonn
alpine.usskiteam.com/athletes/lindsey-vonn
Find out more about Vonn's life here.

Lindsey Vonn
lindseyvonn.com
Learn more about Vonn's career on her official website.

Lindsey Vonn Foundation
lindseyvonnfoundation.org
See what Vonn's charity is doing to help others here.

INDEX